Secrets of French Design

Betty Lou Phillips, ASID

Gibbs Smith, Publisher
Salt Lake City

First Edition
08 07 06 05 04   10 9 8 7 6 5 4 3 2 1

Text © 2004 Betty Lou Phillips
Photographic credits on page 79

Published by
Gibbs Smith, Publisher
P.O. Box 667
Layton, Utah 84041

Orders: 1.800.748.5439
www.gibbs-smith.com

Designed by Cherie Hanson
Printed and bound in Hong Kong

Library of Congress Cataloging-in-Publication Data

Phillips, Betty Lou.
    Secrets of French design / Betty Lou Phillips.— 1st ed.
        p. cm.
    ISBN 1-58685-521-2
    1. Interior decoration—France. I. Title.
    NK2049.A1P48 2004
    747'.0944—dc22
                              2004012783

On the Cover: A silk velvet from the renowned fabric house Scalamandré sprawls across a Louis XVI-style chair by Nancy Corzine. Reportedly, Daisy Fellowes (1887-1962), one of the most glamorous socialites of the time, deserves credit for being the first to recognize the leopard fabric's exotic allure. She used it to cover a sofa. The Scalamandré yellow-and-brown stripe on curtains also merits high praise.

Back Jacket: Glass tiebacks found at the Paris flea market suit elegant Cowtan & Tout silk curtains. Pierre-Auguste Renoir's lithographe Enfants jouant à la balle *graces the boiserie. Table boasts Saint Louis crystal, china from Oustau de Baumanière—in Les Baux village-de-Provence—and Buccellati sterling silver flatware. Toile napkins are from Williams-Sonoma. Floral arrangement by Judy Blackman, Dallas, underscores the dining room's relaxed formality.*

End Papers: Exuding animal magnetism: Scalamandré's leopard silk velvet.

Title Page: Charming in their simplicity are twigs wrapped in rope.

Opposite: The mingling of elegance and ease creates a grand introduction into a maison *brimming with chic decorating ideas. Custom table is by nationally recognized furniture and fabric designer Rose Tarlow for Melrose House, Los Angeles.*

CONTENTS

"The real voyage of discovery consists
not in seeking new landscapes,
but in having new eyes."

—*Marcel Proust*

Preceding Overleaf: Rusticity meets urban sensibility in a room that pays tribute to the owners' style. Milk table is by Rose Tarlow; game table is from Panache. The palette is drawn from the antique Oushak area rug, an Oriental of Turkish origin.

Opposite: A sculpted niche not only offers a place to primp but also dazzles the eye with walls hand painted by Bee Morrow, Decorative Arts, Inc., Houston. Fittings and sink are from Westheimer Plumbing and Hardware, Houston.

Introduction

Given their strong sense of self, commanding flair, and ardor for collecting, to say nothing of their *savoir-faire*, the French simply do not understand American dependence on decorators, which they view as leaving one vulnerable to uncertain results.

Opposite: A handsome hood deserves the spotlight. Each piece of tumbled and pillowed Italian marble—the white is Carrera; the black Negro—is one inch square. The stainless-steel range is by Wolf.

It's not that none would ever dream of collaborating with a design professional, only that most would never turn over control of a project even to the most capable hands. Never mind that ancestral furniture and *objets d'art* conspire to make seeking expert help unnecessary. Most see decorating as an aesthetic undertaking en route to self-satisfaction.

Faced with myriad issues that warrant assistance, the French are likely to have a comprehensive plan, opt to be hands-on, and be exacting in requests—specifying styles, shapes, and proportions in such detail that their wishes leave little doubt.

Yet armed with educated eyes, unerring taste, and amazing confidence, the majority buy what they like, upholding the standards they insist upon while painting flattering self-portraits revealing their passions, interests, and heritage—which is, of course, their intention.

Without fail, settings start with furnishings handed down from one generation to the next. As rooms take shape, they gather even more accoutrements that are meaningful. Determined to prevent their national symbols from fleeing to cities far outside France, habitués flock to the Hôtel Drouot, in Paris's ninth *arrondissement* (district), where three thousand auctions held annually teem with temptations for every predilection.

In addition, they spend weekends relentlessly combing the famous Marché aux Puces de Saint-Ouen, the vast flea market on the outskirts of the capital in existence since 1886, as well as *les puces* (flea markets) at Vanves and Montreuil, unless traipsing to L'Isle-sur-la-Sorgue, the Lubéron's matchless center for antiques,

with more than 250 *brocanteurs* (dealers).

Even so, most interiors are neither cluttered nor intimidating. Despite the grandeur in which Louis XIV resided in the magnificent Palace of Versailles, understated glamour is a design dictum. The French equate elegance with restraint, shunning the Baroque lifestyle identified with the Sun King's reign (1643–1715).

Not that there aren't touches of glamour inside *appartements* in the Ile-de-France—the very heart of France, including Paris and surrounding seven *départements*. Eleven million people live in this historic region. By some estimates, less than twenty-five percent dwell in single family homes.

As it turns out, most apartments are modest in size by American standards, in spite of lofty ceilings, deep chiseled moldings, patterned wood floors, and untold presence. The older the building, in general, the more prestigious it is. Yet, as if a breach of good taste, this is not something residents talk about anymore than those who live behind the heavily lacquered doors leading to eighteenth-and-nineteenth-century *hôtels particuliers*—now divided into apartments—point out that they inhabit the most elegant of all privately owned domains.

Amid the intimacy that classically proportioned rooms afford, unabashedly swirl shimmering taffetas, sophisticated jacquards, smart damasks, and chic chairs from the beguiling rococo period (1730–60) when Louis XV and his renowned mistress, Madame de Pompadour, had great influence on the decorative arts.

And, there is, indeed, nothing conservative about blurry centuries-old mirrors, valued Aubusson carpets, stone busts, and furniture in the style of Louis XVI (1760–89), even if clean-lined neoclassicism developed as a reaction against the perceived excesses of rococo style—about which there is no doubt.

Mixing periods is, of course, common practice, easing formality. But playful leopard fabric may also sweep away the seriousness of a space by making the glamorous appear more relaxed, or vice versa. Certainly, looks vary. Seldom do the French stray from their unified approach to decorating, however.

Whether furnishing an *appartement* on Paris's grand avenue Foch, a *château* in the Loire Valley, or a *bastide* just outside the village of St-Rémy-de-Provence, the French make no secret of their love for family, affection for pets, and fervor for France. But the old-world élan of their rooms may well owe even more to unspoken revelations equally instinctive.

With the wisdom gleaned from fervent beliefs that have long defined French decorating, savvy Americans—designers and not—artfully sculpt satisfying rooms that closely mirror their personalities and the lives they lead.

So what, then, do the French think of the living spaces showcased—drawing on American roots yet owing more than a little to their influence? *C'est impossible* to say. However, we trust that they approve. How could they not? How indeed?

Yet with mystery rooted in the French culture, it is only fitting, perhaps, that their feelings should remain a lasting secret.

Betty Lou Phillips, ASID
Interior Stylist

Opposite: A toile from Lee Jofa wraps a room and a nineteenth-century iron daybed in understated beauty. At the time, horsehair or wadded cotton would have filled the cushion. Here, delft vases circa 1830 rest on English hand-carved wall brackets from Jas A. Gundry, Inc., Houston. Hovering over the bed are Minton, Canova, and Dresden patterned plates, soup bowls, and platters—all equally alluring.

Les Couleurs de France

Taking a cue from the land, the sun, and the glistening Mediterranean Sea, not established trend forecasters, interiors echo the splendor of France the way Mother Nature intended, many say.

Fine furnishings and fabrics venture outdoors as the "Louis Soleil Collection" for Sutherland —on Regal Row in Dallas—makes its debut. Nickel-plated, weather-resistant, stainless steel nailheads adorn an al fresco Perennials stripe. The hand-carved teak frame—designed by award-winning John Hutton—is offered in numerous weathered finishes.

Blue—once believed to keep all manner of misfortune away—lands in a wave of favorite shades, from the sapphire blue that bathes the sweeping coastline to the sky blue in the cloudless countryside to the violet blue of lavender beds faded by the sun. Splashes of balmy yellow, poppy red, and deeper claret shore up sites flooded with light, winning admiration, too.

Color also makes its way from faithfully tended vineyards, olive groves, and wheat fields, as well as orchards with the latest crop of peaches and plums. As if that weren't enough, the shifting shades of leafy green offer even more decorating choices.

Finally, in a country entrenched in its fabled past, mellow old-world shades of ochre—whose pigments range from oxblood with undertones of brown to pale yellow—are coaxed from the earth into rooms where they vie for the right to have their say. Not that the color is limited to interiors—hardly. Seventeen

painterly shades—including sienna, umber, and, not least, terra-cotta—swathe houses in the Lubéron village of

visual interest and drama, straying beyond conventional combinations to more distinctive, unexpected choices,

While the color wheel is a universal tool thought helpful in pairing hues, the French maintain that world authorities cannot improve on nature whose endless color possibilities coexist in harmony.

Roussillon, whose rolling hills are an important resource for ochre sold around the globe.

While the color wheel is a universal tool considered helpful in pairing hues, the French maintain that world authorities cannot improve on nature, whose endless color possibilities coexist in harmony. As proof, they offer a chic mix of

after focusing on the use of the room and changing light, both natural and artificial.

No matter that more than a century ago French chemist Michel Eugène Chevreul's pioneering work as director of Gobelin, the famous tapestry and carpeting manufacturer, contributed to the development of the color wheel. Given that France's climate and terrain vary from region to region, most people prefer trusting their instincts—drawing color from nature's schemes or the façades of historic sites.

Intense, saturated Mediterranean hues that can hold their own in the glaring sun fill dwellings in the South of France, where subdued tones can look lifeless and dull. By contrast, vibrant colors appear garish in Paris, which sits at about the same latitude as Seattle, and where a more formal, yet relaxed, spirit often pervades without splashes of gilding.

In the French capital as well as other places with moody weather, posh muted shades such as oatmeal, parchment, putty, and taupe project gracious, sophisticated airs that are anything but drab. Mixing subtle values of the same color appeals to the uptown sensibilities of Parisians, whose cosmopolitan style requires that wall finishes, fabrics, and furnishings simply complement each other rather than court attention.

In the pursuit of beauty, some scrape centuries of paint off walls, trying to unearth the original color, or at least one suggestive of what once was. Dozens more see no need to make any changes to a place filled with memories. Since most dwellings remain in the same family for generations, all see the charm in paying homage to the past while embracing the palette of France.

Translated, an old French proverb proclaims, "A white wall is the fool's paper," not taking into account the hundreds of paint chips on the market that people might be left obsessing over—actually, enough to make some stick with white.

In a serendipitous turn, however, the adage also deserves credit for publicizing the power of color, which can make authoritative statements, alter outlooks, and help shrug off stress. It also can solve some irksome design problems—without moving walls, raising roofs, adding on, or making other structural improvements, which, in this world of uncertainty, is equally impressive.

It is a stretch to say, however, that any adage would ever hold the French hostage. Those who don't subscribe to its view are quick to point out that white contains a spectrum of colors that change with the light, causing a room to appear gray at one time of day, green another. But even they readily acknowledge that to increase the sense of space, highlight admirable architecture, and quell ceiling shortcomings, it is worth adopting the following guidelines that make a room more inviting:

❧ Light, less-than-intense cool colors— for instance, blue and green—make walls recede, giving quarters lacking square footage a far more spacious feel.

❧ Dark, warm colors—red, orange, and yellow—do just the opposite. Advancing hues work overtime making generously sized rooms appear more intimate by absorbing light.

Opposite: A Pierre Deux toile lures hues from the South of France into a guest room. The trundle bed is new and the trunk antique.

❦ Rich, sun-drenched colors look best after dark lit by candles, picture lights, wall sconces, and carefully placed table and floor lamps, with dimmer switches adjusting lighting levels. During the day, deep colors accentuate cracks and patches on walls, as well as make ceiling imperfections difficult to ignore.

❦ Daring, sizzling hues are worth thinking twice about, should the whim strike, unless one is living in a region with saturated light that blatantly demands colors as brilliant as the sun.

❦ Walls and molding with minimum contrast—which means the latter painted just slightly deeper than the former—fashionably disguise nondescript trim and other surfaces lacking architectural panache, such as radiators. Avoiding visual rivalry also brings the illusion of height to a low-ceiling room. Some argue, knowingly, that mixing one-third to one-half a can of wall color to two-thirds to one-half a can of white perceptibly elevates a ceiling to even greater heights.

❦ Conversely, a ceiling painted the same color as the walls seemingly lowers the ceiling. So, too, does painting it darker than the walls.

❦ In spaces with sufficient light, a subtle shade of white works well as a frame for contrasting walls.

❦ Garrets are not a place to experiment with bold, eye-popping colors, even when bathed in light. The same serene shade on walls and ceiling masks odd contours, increases the feeling of space, and leaves a room feeling tranquil, which is indeed the goal.

❦ Enveloping walls and sloping ceilings in a small-scale patterned paper also creates an air of spaciousness that matches the mood of the times.

❦ Glazing—a decorative painting technique whose quiet sheen colors a painted surface and adds depth—calls attention to crown molding and skirting worthy of praise. Whether or not the color contrasts with the walls, glazing is a necessary step to project the sought-after patina of age, many contend.

❦ Trompe l'oeil—an optical illusion that does its utmost to delight the heart and arouse curiosity—makes a flat surface appear three-dimensional. In French, *tromper* means "to deceive or to trick"; *l'oeil*, "the eye."

APPRECIATION
FOR TEXTURE

A room with few textures pro-
duces the feeling of space. But in the
minds of the French, a fluid mix is
far more pleasing and a pleasure
worth pursuing, considering that a
setting with all sleek finishes is
unavoidably cold, while texture
results in triumphant warmth.

As it happens, texture has a reputa-
tion for shaping rooms much as color,
whose opposites attract. Yet, integrating
disparate materials can be awkward,
mostly because layering furniture, fabrics,
and lighting requires pulling together
more than myriad variations of rough
and smooth. Unless contrasting finishes
create the feeling of well-being, a setting
can be jarringly off-putting—more
shocking than charming.

*Venturing beyond the usual, a Louis Philippe clothing rack
with cane inlay, dated 1845, puts a fashionable spin on a hall-
way wall.*

In those awash in the signature extremes—light and heavy, hard and soft, coarse and shiny, refined and relaxed—harmony is the ultimate goal. Whether expressing passion for the *ancien régime* or a taste for Napoléon III and Empress Eugénie's eclectic, overstuffed Second Empire (1852–70) splendor, French artistry demands juxtaposing soft, sensuous surfaces among those perceived severe—the more subtly, the better.

Here's how the French do just that and then some:

❧ Faithful to their heritage, exquisitely fashioned, hand-forged railings wrap balconies and staircases, which is hardly surprising, given that the French gift for making magnificent objects from iron is well known.

❧ Unassuming fireplaces, worn wood floors—sometimes laid in a herringbone pattern—and handsome, heavy doors clad in original fittings, unpretentiously speak for themselves.

❧   In rooms with high ceilings, exposed wood beams fuse the warmth and charm of rural France with the unmistakably urbane sensibilities of Paris, conveying the feeling of a country house far from the capital.

❧ Glazing lends an old-world aura to textured, hand-plastered walls, by reflecting light differently than paint depending on the base and top coats used. White walls layered in translucent biscuit, for instance, give the appearance of worn parchment. (For walls that lack character, American Clay Plaster in Albuquerque, New Mexico offers a formula easily mixed with water and troweled over most any primed surface including textured ceilings and old paint. Twelve standard colors imitate rough Provençal plaster or Venetian plaster.)

❦ Venetian plaster—another decorative finish favorite—borrows alluring tints such as dove, ivory, and champagne from the luminosity of eighteenth-century silks, thus bestowing character.

❦ Since dramatic textures attract more than their fair share of attention, most Parisians use them sparingly, perhaps offering a clue why today more people favor painted rather than splashy gilded furniture. Or why area rugs are more popular than carpeting running wall to wall.

❦ Domestic furnishings are the norm. But a widely held attraction for hand-painted Italian country desks and commodes makes both increasingly difficult to find.

❦ Reflective surfaces— crystal chandeliers, antique mirrors, and French forties coffee tables among them—multiple the light and city views. After being ignored for most of the twentieth century— mostly because they harbored memories of war and the German occupation of France (1940–44)—furnishings from the 1940s now outshine many collectables, recently prompting the French firm Pierre Frey to introduce a forties-inspired fabric collection. Mercury lamps and *verre-églomisé* vases (painted on the reverse side of the glass) also radiate fresh modernity.

❦ Cut velvets make a bold statement, defining what it means to be fashionable.

able light, communicating an elegant, uptown spirit that complements deep moldings and elegantly carved *boiserie* glazed light gray, gray-green, or gray-blue.

❦ Posh fabrics—some from the grand house of Braquenié—also rise to the occasion, tempering the stuffiness of oak-paneled *boiserie,* while casting parquet de Versailles floors and antique urns turned

Glazing lends an old-world aura to textured, hand-plastered walls, by reflecting light differently than paint depending on the base and top coats used.

❦ Sumptuous silk-taffeta curtains—or window treatments in other fabrics with a glossy finish—catch avail-

into lamps in new light with a gamut of stylish shades.

❦ Soft, nubby weaves such as chenille, corduroy, twill, tweed, and wool cast shadows that absorb light, much like advancing hues. Although warm and

❦ Clearly, there isn't much chintz in Parisian flats. Nor are there many bold florals. Stripes, spots, plaids, and checks bring pizzazz to relaxed areas, though

Though often perceived as poor relations of their more refined neighbors, the humble sit across from the grand, the ordinary across from the extraordinary unobtrusively imparting French flair yet making it clear that good taste is not about personal wealth or visual extravagance.

welcoming, they appear casual, regardless of the colorway.

the look depends upon their scale and the most prominent textile.

❦ Natural linens in nature-inspired hues also evoke a carefree manner. And cottons even more so; plain or patterned, they do the same.

❦ Authentically French, monochromatic toiles de Jouy (pronounced twälz-da-'zhwee) grace furniture, lamp shades, and walls. Story-telling rural and mythological etched scenes—printed in sepia, red, violet, aubergine, or indigo on the finest cotton ground—originated in the eighteenth century Oberkampf factory in the town of Jouy-en-Josas, near Versailles.

❦ Color-drenched cotton prints called *indiennes*—first produced in seventeenth-century India and then imported to France, look right at home in laid-back Provence. In Parisian circles, seldom are they seen.

❦ An eighteenth-century fascination with China led to a fondness for chinoiserie, which remains *en vogue* to this day. The curved shapes of fish, birds, flowers, and pagodas offset harsher lines.

❦ Whether adorning the skirt of a sofa, an ottoman, or a chair, nothing softens tailored silhouettes like deep bullion fringe. It also dresses up a room.

❦ Without looking as if it is trying, fringe mitigates hard edges on throw pillows while camouflaging seams and zippers, which are hardly chic.

❦ Though often perceived as poor relations of their more refined neighbors, the humble sit across from the grand, the ordinary across from the extraordinary, unobtrusively imparting French flair yet making it clear that good taste is not about personal wealth or visual extravagance.

❦ Mellow wood pieces with warm, varied patinas promote the image that a setting has evolved over time. Simultaneously, they ground a room with light walls.

❦ While two wood pieces sitting side by side gives rise to the sense that something is amiss, fabric separating wood finishes erases any hint of a rivalry.

❦ Most important, finishes need space to breathe. Seemingly, only then can texture influence the character of a room in a positive way.

Le Salon

Le salon par excellence is, indeed, a work of art, inspired by France's storied culture and splendid architecture. Most often, however, tangible links to caring ancestors who lived centuries apart make the most abiding impression.

Opposite: A chic living room with furnishings crafted in eighteenth- and nineteenth-century France exudes glamour at its twenty-first-century best. Stenciled walls have the faded look of antique textiles.

Unlike family cast-offs that dwell in American homes only until we can afford to replace and easily forget them, the French treat long-adored furnishings as pieces of history fit to reign forever in the most coveted spots.

But, then, who could begrudge a regal armoire, the celebrated source of Gallic pride, the opportunity to pay homage to France with its magnificence? Built in the thirteenth-century for storing armor, the armoire has risen to iconic status since becoming emblematic of French country life.

Variations abound, though some stand apart. Most prized of all are those with deep carving, shaped tops, and the patina of age—the distinctive luster resulting from centuries of exposure to heat, humidity, and light, to say nothing of oil from loving hands, being that the first thing people often do is touch a piece of furniture. Yet, even an armoire that might not ordinarily merit a second look can lend a bit of grandeur when privy to a well-documented pedigree or tales of its meanderings.

No matter that it inevitably overshadows other elements in the room. For centuries, the French have favored large-scale furnishings of noble propor-

spacious apartments, it stands to reason that furniture would still have the imposing look expected when the custom of handing down family heirlooms remains unchanged.

Predictably, then, the armoire isn't the only heirloom reestablishing its pre-eminence. Rock-crystal (colorless

For centuries, the French have favored large-scale furnishings of noble proportions. Even in small rooms, generously sized furnishings look stately, not stuffy.

tions. Even in small rooms, generously sized furnishings look stately, not stuffy. And, how could it be otherwise? As large *châteaux* throughout France have given rise to smaller *maisons* and less-

quartz) chandeliers, *trumeaux* (painted overmantels), and screens with painted scenes offer the reassuring feel of the familiar while making dramatic statements. Age-old tapestries peering

A tight view of stenciled walls on page 32, by Houston artist Bee Morrow.

down from walls paint *salons* with further importance.

In those that want for nothing, chairs
of different sizes and ages are tell-tale
signs that sites have evolved over time.
Matching ensembles—namely anything
indistinguishable from the next, including five-piece place settings of the same
china and pairs of side tables—hold no
interest. Nor, it seems, do many repro-
ductions of originals.

With insistence on quality inherent
in French genes, people are remarkably
disciplined—capable of living for years
without a rug, tapestry, commode or
other object of desire until one that is
truly loved comes along, meaning one
finely crafted, with presence, and the
patina of age. To their way of thinking, it
is inexcusable to live in a house full of

meaningless pieces with no ties to the past, and even worse, one furnished at a hurried pace with pricey objects lacking character.

In bygone eras, imperial-looking *récamiers*, settees, *bergères* (fully upholstered armchairs with enclosed sides and exposed wood frames), *fauteuils* (upholstered armchairs with open sides) stiffly hugged the perimeter of a room. These days, artfully grouped seating—including ottomans and chaise lounges parked in front of fireplaces—makes it easy for a people with a passion for intellectualizing and appreciation for the decorative arts to discuss most anything, including pressing concerns. Ingrained in polite society is an aversion to talking about personal finances or materialistic attachments, however.

While some people prefer letting bare parquet de Versailles or stone put on their own floor show, others are drawn to the beauty of hand-loomed Orientals. Most, though, favor timeworn Savonnerie area rugs, once woven for royalty, and faded Aubussons with their tapestry-like weave that add an air of dignity.

Yet with the country's 10 million dogs, or one for every six citizens, clearly having the run of houses, practicality is often a weighty consideration influencing design choices.

Nostalgia aside, durable sisal sprawled across hardwood floors suggests a laissez-faire lifestyle. Humble jute, coir, and sea grass—used for centuries—also epitomize today's easy ways. Not everyone loves natural grass

Opposite: Light pours into a library where old-world comfort and warmth meet and a leather chair holds sway. There is no doubt that this room differs from the one where French novelist Victor Hugo (1802-50) wrote The Hunchback of Notre Dame *and* Les Misérables.

rugs, however. Dozens find the texture too abrasive for bare feet and infants' knees, causing it to lose some of its cachet.

Tailored slipcovers with lush detailing—piping, corner pleats, and flat rather than frilly skirts—aim to protect seating with luxurious fabrics and impressive detailing hidden underneath. For that matter, they also camouflage weary furniture, giving pieces a fresh look far less expensively than replacing or reupholstering. At their intimate best, they fit sofas, chairs, and ottomans *perfectly.*

Even tightly edited spaces host heroic-sized family portraits and photographs in frames, freshly cut flowers arranged *en masse,* and well-read books heaped high on coffee tables that are roomy enough to hold chess boards.

Sturdy side tables that withstand the rigors of playful, ever-present dogs offer places for wine glasses, plates of cheese and *pâtés,* and magazines. Always there are plump pillows—stitched from various vintage textiles—to rest against and throws draped in a romantic fashion, not by chance.

With the obsession for detail for which they are legendary, the French have a seemingly endless ability to make decorating appear effortless—an attribute not easy to come by—particularly for a people deliberate in their thinking.

Central to the salons that harbor them, billowing window treatments screen unappealing views, guard privacy, filter direct sunlight, and, not least, solicit admiring glances. With or without dangling *passementerie* (trimming and tassels) cascading down leading edges, they hang as glamorously as exquisitely constructed ball gowns, dazzling the eye while revealing the French's celebrated fascination with beauty.

Until not so long ago, most every Parisian apartment with parquet de Versailles floors and *portes fenêtres* (floor-to-ceiling windows) that resemble doors, resounded with grandiose curtains that not only seemed to outweigh some segments of the population but also did more for the fabled textile mills hidden outside Lyon than imagined. No more.

In a sign of the times, perhaps, settings appear less opulent lately.

Conspicuously missing are elaborate over-the-top cornices hovering above windows, swags (fabric lengths spilling in front of the glass), and jabots (side pieces framing the pane) that many people nowadays consider the height of pretension and a bit much for rooms with precious little floor space. Even valences—certainly a staple in English country houses—are becoming passé. Like cornices, they have a way of visually lowering ceilings, not to mention making windows appear shorter than they are.

These days, fabrics framing towering doors and windows plunge from ceiling to floor, exalting simplicity. Yes, some curtains with utmost style tumble from eye-catching gilded poles accompanied by carved finials worthy of the past. But still more descend quietly from iron rods and rings. Although points of view vary

on rod placement, one glance confirms that the smartest curtains fall from as close to the ceiling molding as possible, making even small rooms look somewhat grander.

Dressmaker headings run the gamut from pencil pleats whose narrow columns create fullness, to fancier pleats pinched at the top, to painstakingly smocked headings where stitched latticework creates a pattern. What makes all exceptionally alluring are some essential characteristics:

❦ To preserve natural light, curtains extend beyond the width of the window twelve to fifteen inches on each side, unfailingly mirroring the scale of the room rather than upsetting its proportions.

❦ For *très* chic richness, workrooms ceremoniously calculate fabric at

two-and-a-half—and more often than not, three—times the distance from one end of the curtain rod to the other, including returns—the space from the face of the rod to the wall. There's no skimping on fabric. What's more, the French freely confess that they are not apt to purchase expensive textiles and then fabricate curtains themselves.

❦ Light streaming in windows silhouettes the beauty of lace. But when it comes to airy sheers or gauzy fabrics that the French call *voilage*—voile, organdy, muslin, batiste—quadrupling a window's width insures privacy.

❦ *Au courant* stripes—which Napoléon loved to tout—make their own fashion statement while luring ceilings into appearing taller than reality.

Opposite: A tight of library curtains with dash.

❧ Working together, lining and hidden interlining block light, absorb sound, help prevent sun damage, and turn a casual window treatment into couture. But an unexpected lining—such as an irresistible plaid taffeta peeking from behind a solid silk or wool—alone, adds surprising splendor.

hardwoods invariably create niches for pampered pooches to sleep. Regardless, the French scoff at curtains that stop short!

❧ *Passementerie*—rooted in fashion—rouses interest. Tassels hark back to the time of the ancient Egyptians, when they spared embarrassment by

Though not as showy as their fringe cousins, braids and tapes supply artful, finished borders with striking individuality.

❧ Lest one wonder: Weights stitched in deep, deep hems insure that curtains drape gracefully and then turn under in soft folds.

❧ Curtains simply brush the floor or "break" no more than three inches. It seems those that "puddle" on

snugly keeping royal robes in place. These days, elegant tiebacks and trims have nothing to do with modesty.

❧ Though not as showy as their fringe cousins, braids and tapes supply artful, finished borders with striking individuality.

❧ Narrow piping running down leading edge and streaming across the floor eliminates the need to justify the cost of tempting trim. In the words of twentieth-century tastemaker Sister Parish, "Curtains must always have an edge or an ending," trumpeting a principle of French design that American designers never tire of repeating.

❧ In French eyes, less-than-perfectly-straight seams, a pattern that fails to match, or fringe sewn in a questionable manner is any window treatment's undoing.

❧ Handsome natural shades are in keeping with today's less-is-more look, or a yearning for minimalism.

❧ Dressed up or even dressed down, Roman shades block the sun's rays and soften windows where curtains would get in the way or simply look like black holes at night. Those mounted with inside brackets draw attention to impressive molding, while shades mounted outside the casing—as close to the ceiling molding as possible—make a window look larger without obstructing either the light or view.

❧ As if to push a short window to the limit, mounting a Roman shade under the curtains gives the window presence. Once again, the guiding rule seems to be that both should be mounted as close to the ceiling as possible.

❧ Contrary to expectations, suddenly, balloon shades have joined the ranks of over-the-top window treatments—seldom welcome anywhere.

THE FINE ART OF EXHIBITING ART

With its renowned museums and highly respected art galleries, Paris has long been a paradise for art lovers and artists. It wasn't until 1850, though, that the first gallery opened. Earlier, struggling artists faced the daunting task of finding venues where they could exhibit their work. The needs of those in the art world spurred France's art schools, better known as *academies*, to hold annual and sometimes semiannual exhibitions, or *salons.*

Among the most esteemed was the Paris *salon*, where artists selected by a jury jostled for recognition on soaring walls stacked high with art. Since capturing visitors' attention virtually assured demand for an artist's work, competition was fierce for coveted eye-level spots.

Reportedly, the jury dismissed artists Pierre-Auguste Renoir, Claude Monet, Alfred Sisley, Jean Bazille, Camille Pissarro, Paul Cézanne, and Edouard Manet, whose distinctive, unorthodox way of capturing light *en plein-air* went against established tastes. To appease them, Napoléon III (1852–70) founded the now-famous *"Salon des Refusés,"* (Salon of the Refused), in 1863, which encouraged the French and others to view the Impressionists with new understanding, thus shifting public perception, albeit reluctantly.

Nevertheless, to this day Europeans stack paintings and drawings high on walls and over doors in a manner called salon style. Meanwhile, on this side of the Atlantic, works of art loom in a

Opposite: Mixing the humble and the grand, Flemish paintings grace a powder room's walls. Giving new meaning to unassuming, Dallas decorative artists Joe Mear and Kim Morgan covered the walls with grocery sacks, then applied overlays of metallic tempera paint. The commode is antique.

modern fashion—that is, in a single row surrounded by ample space.

Some of the strongest groupings mass similar subjects—say landscapes, ladies, children, fruit, animals, birds, flowers, not to mention tightly arranged botanicals or architectural plates—creating a focus of their own.

Either way, displaying works of art is an art in itself, much harder than it looks, even for a people seemingly having a sixth sense for style. It is hardly any wonder, then, that the French borrow tips from none other than their famous museums that offer timeless lessons in placing art, any more than that they add a few ideas of their own:

❧ Paintings make a stronger impression when congregated together, hung inches apart, rather than scattered around the room.

❧ Some of the strongest groupings mass similar subjects—say, landscapes, ladies, children, fruit, animals, birds, flowers, not to mention tightly arranged botanicals or architectural plates—creating a focus of their own. This is not to say that collections must be single-minded to fuse seamlessly; only that a sole subject offers an organizing principle.

❧ Indeed, decking a wall with a thought-provoking composition of oil paintings, watercolors, gouaches, and drawings can shape a single arrangement.

- Large or small, a work of art that eclipses the rest— in value or in sentiment—is worthy of pride of place at the center of a grouping, readily drawing the attention of those entering the room. The honor is a testament to its significance.

- A small painting hung beneath a larger one arouses interest. Naturally, it is best to view some artwork at a distance, other work close up.

- Different-sized frames arranged in a rectangle—either horizontal or vertical—create a sense of order. (In horizontal groupings with a modern twist, an imaginary line separates two rows: the bottoms of the top row of frames hang in a straight line, and the top of frames in the lower row form a straight line.

Generally, between the rows, there is about eight inches of space. In a vertical grouping, the outer edges of frames line up.)

- Many museums insist on pairing works with frames from the same period. Not that this is an easy thing to do. It is rare to find age-appropriate frames in the flea markets, mostly because not many survived the French Revolution, much less two world wars.

- A frame should never overshadow the art. Then again, an impressive frame can garner added respect for a less-than-important work of art by giving it a stronger presence.

- For pared-down simplicity, a stretched canvas can hang frameless against a backdrop of dramatic architecture.

❦ An ancestral portrait need not be by Elisabeth Louise Vigée Le Brun (1755–1842), Queen Marie Antoinette's favorite portraitist, to perch on an antique easel. Most any generous painting can offset a tall wood piece across the room or interrupt the line of furniture all the same height.

❦ The idea of propping paintings on fireplaces reaches back to seventeenth-century England. At the time, lofty gilt mirrors hung above smoke-stained chimneypieces in France's grandiosely paneled rooms, coloring the capital's gray light. Sometimes *boiserie* had oil paintings inset. Paintings also adorned the tall, narrow spaces between windows, as they still do. But these days, works of art often stand on fireplaces, too.

❦ The French are ever mindful that direct sunlight never falls on prints, watercolors, or textiles. Fading, yellowing, and foxing can result from overexposure to light; heat can crack oil paintings.

❦ Although not all works of art need be illuminated in identical ways, low-voltage picture lights often hang above paintings in France. Meanwhile, lighting has gone high-tech in museums and homes here in the United States.

Opposite: The French traditionally receive and entertain guests in le salon, *where style flows from a penchant for detail.*

A Table

While we find it difficult to curb an appetite for the latest stainless-steel commercial ranges and glass-front refrigerators to complement wine coolers stocked with fine champagne, most all the staples of high-style performance these days are missing in French kitchens.

Opposite: With the charm of rural France, a cypress mantel—stained and distressed to resemble antique pine—hovers over a Viking stovetop. The carved wooden plaque de chasse aux oiseaux *depicts French fowl.*

Appliances sit in plain sight. There are no granite countertops or family-friendly islands touting togetherness, let alone twenty-first-century computer centers lauded for their own prowess.

Noticeably absent, too, are paneled upper cabinet doors. Instead, open shelves brim with pitchers, pottery, glassware, platters, trays, and other paraphernalia illustrating just how passionate the French are about their cuisine.

Unlike Americans, who tend to tuck clutter out of sight in designated cabinets, the French prefer that cutting boards, *porte couverts* (cutlery holders with knives that carve, chop, pare, peel, and dice), richly glazed confit pots, small appliances, and baskets for storing fresh bread vie for counter space with collections of tin molds: some for baking, some for chocolate making, and some to satisfy cravings for sorbet or ice cream.

Windowsills meanwhile, flaunt mossy pots of sage, rosemary, chives, and basil.

There's no question that French kitchens can rightly boast of being incredibly efficient—with an array of world in on the merits of copper—or at least selling the younger generation on the notion.

As if on cue, hardwood floors sweep uninterrupted from dining rooms in some

In a country long the uncontested capital of haute cuisine most kitchens are surprisingly small, thanks to everything from being more about cooking than socializing to resistance to change from the time when they were servants' domains to homeowners who perhaps lack significant sums to invest in expanding and improving their kitchens.

equipment designed to steam, strain, boil, and drain within easy reach.

Scores of pans, colanders, and bowls in every size imaginable crowd *crémaillères* (pot racks), as if letting the regions. Sleek black-and-white tile lends distinction in others. Far from an afterthought, unglazed, oversized squares or octagons of terra-cotta tile have the flavor of Provence, Burgundy, and the Loire

Opposite: A stainless-steel showpiece stocks most all the utensils a serious cook needs.

Valley, where clay is plentiful and there's ample charm.

In a country long the uncontested capital of *haute cuisine*, most kitchens are surprisingly small, thanks to everything from being more about cooking than socializing, to resisting change from the time when they were servants' domains, to homeowners who perhaps lack significant sums to invest in expanding and improving their kitchens. By comparison, Americans spent $214 billion in 2003 chasing renovation dreams, according to the National Association of the Remodeling Industry.

Custom painted-vegetable sink in the island of kitchen shown on page 50.

LE CROISSANT

Legends abound. One of Austria's most celebrated—early one morning in 1683, while fashioning decadent creations, Viennese bakers heard strange noises and alerted authorities, who discovered that the Turks were tunneling underneath Vienna—and credited the bakers with saving the city. To the latter, it seemed symbolically fitting that people would enjoy devouring the enemy. So, extracting the crescent—or *croissant*, in French—from the Turkish flag, the bakers shaped their dough.

More certain: Nearly a century later, in 1770, Princess Marie-Antoinette—sent from her native Austria to marry the future Louis XVI —introduced the *croissant* to France.

Today, *boulangeries* sell all kinds of bread, including the *croissant* and the baguette. *Patisseries* sell pastries.

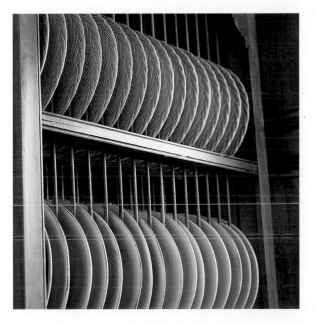

Inspired by the charm of the classic French kitchen, glazed earthenware it is not sandwiched into cupboards.

When the French entertain, impeccably bedecked tables overflow with sparkling crystal, oversize linen napkins, resplendent well-polished silver, and a striking mix of heirloom china patterns, setting the stage for candlelight fêtes designed to please the senses as much as the palate.

By common consent, perhaps, the handle of each piece of sterling silver flatware sits near the table's edge, while the dessert spoon and fork lie above the plate. In keeping with the French mind-

set, the dessert spoon rests closest to the plate's rim, with its handle to the right, as if hinting that it may join the other spoons on the right side of the plate. Above the dessert spoon lays the dessert fork, with its handle to the left.

Unlike other cultures, the tines of forks face down, resting on the table

cloth—a custom that some say developed to undercut the fork's ability to snag ruffled lace sleeves. Others claim someone thought the tines of forks and bowls of spoons looked less aggressive

Unlike other cultures, the tines of forks face down—resting on the table cloth—a that custom some say developed to undercut the fork's ability to snag ruffled lace sleeves.

Opposite: The influence of the French moves from the kitchen on page 50 into an inviting nook, where a farm table, circa 1870 from Carl Moore Antiques, Houston, rests on an Aubusson from Stark Carpet. A mix of pretty fabrics covers skirted host chairs (one unseen).

faced down, saying nothing about drawing attention to engraved initials without being obvious. But in fairness, the flip sides liberally borrow flourishes from various chapters in French history and often are even more decorative.

Centerpieces are always low—with fresh flowers straight from the garden or from local markets—so they do not interfere with conversations. Indeed, in France there is an unwritten rule: talk must continue even after a lingering

Centerpieces are always low—with fresh flowers straight from the garden or from local markets—so they do not interfere with conversation.

Water and wine goblets meet directly above each plate, rather than above the knife and spoon as in the States. A regal "underplate" called a charger by Americans, is integral to the table's beauty; it is removed before the first course is served.

meal followed by dessert. For one to simply pick up and leave without engaging in further conversation is considered socially incorrect, insinuating that a dinner party is thought less than successful.

Opposite: A sophisticated bookcase of Italian descent–from Hermitage Antiques, Dallas–holds a pleasing mix of antiques, including a collection of confit jars. The walnut dining table is from Michael Taylor, Los Angeles.

In the United States, sterling is 925 parts silver to 75 parts copper, honoring the universally accepted norm established in the fourteenth century and still accepted worldwide today. While it is treated with respect here in America, the French are less than enamored with second standard silver—a term that refers to the ratio of purity in pieces marked with the numeral two.

Since the eighteenth century, first standard silver—composed of 950 parts silver to 50 parts copper and adorned with the numeral one—has been a notable source of French pride while garnering an international roster of admirers intent on passing it down for eternity. Some pieces bear the maker's personal stamp. But the hallmark always reveals the district where crafted, while the control mark bespeaks the year it was produced.

It was Napoléon who set uniform silver marks throughout France, beginning with the *Coq* (rooster), followed by the *Vieillard* (old man), which gave way to the head of Minerva in 1838.

Now as then, sterling ages gracefully unless called into service only on holidays, while stainless flatware becomes duller with use. And though French flatware is larger than that produced in America, one doesn't feel its heaviness, thanks to its design.

Opposite: All that glitters is not gold—at least not at this table set in the French style. From the venerable house of Christofle, founded in 1830, comes "Malmaison" sterling flatware, crystal, and porcelain. The silver charger, or "underplate," as it is known in France, is "Beauharnais." The Empress Josephine purchased Malmaison—a retreat outside Paris—while Napoléon was in Egypt in 1799.

La Chambre

Back in the eighteenth century, the bedroom was where high level meetings took place—until Madame de Pompadour, the most famous of Louis XV's mistresses, removed her *chambre* from the list of public rooms.

Gathering the trappings of an enviable lifestyle around her, she announced that privacy was the ultimate luxury. Then, in a quiet revolution, she boldly sealed her quarters from uninvited glares. Only then did her bedroom become worthy of being called a boudoir, fulfilling its promise as a place to pout or sulk.

The head-spinning ascension of Jeanne-Antoinette Poisson from modest beginnings as wife of a Parisian tax farmer to irresistible mistress stunned the royal court. Though Madame de Pompadour professed not to notice, detractors called her "fish face" behind her back, since in French *poisson* means fish. Nothing suggested that the protocol she set in place would forever alter Gallic bedroom culture, yet all of France followed her example.

Nowadays, etiquette dictates that a bedroom door must

remain shut, both day and night. Also, it is poor manners for a person to peer into another person's *chambre,* whether or not someone is in the room. Almost always, the French close the shutters adorning their homes at night, much like Americans might hang a sign on the

levels of splendor fueled an array of variations.

As befitting a majestic mansion, Madame de Pompadour and Louis XV's love swirled in a *lit à la française* (canopied bed)—with a crown presiding overhead. Opulent bed hangings billowed romanti-

No different from the time of the ancient Egyptians, eighteenth-century beds were the ultimate symbols of wealth.

door requesting "Privacy." It is also unheard of to purchase a bedroom suite with wood finishes boringly alike.

No different from the time of the ancient Egyptians, eighteenth-century beds were the ultimate symbols of wealth. As a result, rivalry for matchless

cally, creating a luxurious room within a room when untied.

To this day, the French lavish extraordinary attention on their beds. Most all sheets are white or ecru and posh Egyptian cotton, if not 100 percent linen, which becomes softer and whiter with

Opposite: The sitting area in a master bedroom offers a suggestion for preserving memorable moments. The settee is in the style of Louis XV. The chairs (one unseen) are Louis Philippe period pieces, dating to 1840.

age. Not hampered by thread count, which people say can be misleading beyond a soft 340 threads per square inch, there is awareness of the comfort bedding offers and the amenities of splendor: embroidery, appliqué, and applied laces. Those not inclined to compromise their standards covet long, thin, single-ply fibers for extra softness and durability, and pillowcases with an interior flap that not only hides the pillow from view but also helps keep it in place.

Borrowing a glamorous mix of style and drama from eras past, a dressing table may add to the setting's allure. *La table de toilette* actually made its debut late in the eighteenth century. Historians say that Madame de Pompadour ceremoniously encouraged courtiers seeking the king's favor to present themselves at an hour when she would be *à la toilette*. Feeling that she looked especially attractive at that time enticed her to abandon her need for privacy.

These days, a boudoir is as likely to serve as a spot for corresponding as for sleeping, so it typically includes a writing table. And, though area rugs often grace spaces, bare floors are common, too. Seldom do the French lay carpet. What's more, closets are rare. In fact, some say that armoires owe their enduring esteem to satisfying the need for storage space in rooms.

BED CULTURE

While one might think twice about shipping a bed from a Paris flea market, there's no reason not to consider adopting France's artfully layered bed culture when searching for a good night's rest. In a twist on tradition, it goes against the natural order of things, paying the rest of Europe little mind.

Apart from what one sees, a stuffed and quilted mattress pad tops the mattress, followed by two flat sheets, then a blanket covered by another sheet. During the coolest months, a *couette* (comforter) filled with *duvet* (down) that comes from the underbellies of geese—eiderdown fill is ultralight and the priciest—traps the warmth. Come morning, the French fold *les couettes* at the foot of the bed.

In the French mind, a bed is not complete without *un traversin*—a long, firm, round bolster spanning the mattress's width. Often it is wrapped in a blanket cover; always it supports European square pillows. The middle sheet reveals a monogram or the family crest applied so that it can be readily read by a person standing at the foot of the bed.

Taking a walk back in time, monograms began as efficient laundry marks—often hand stitched in colorfast red—that made a concerted effort to insure that freshly washed linens returned to their rightful owners. They moved to places of honor in nineteenth-century Victorian hope chests awaiting impending marriages. But long before then, nuns, who learned the art as children, elegantly hand embroidered ornate lettering on church vestments.

Actually, by the mid-sixteenth century, the taste for monogrammed table and bed linens reached royal residences and then added a layer of respectability to dwelling beyond. Fancy or not, personalized linens were refined extensions of oneself, much like a signature deliberately crafted reinforces a stylish image. For each letter formed part of the next, as if intent on making a lasting impression by remaining forever intertwined.

Still, Diane de Poitiers, mistress of Henri II (1519–59) somehow managed to alter the official monogram of the French king and his queen, Catherine de Medici (1519–89), changing the intertwined H and C to H and D.

Today, monograms no longer are the domain of the rich and noble, of course. But they are regal indulgences, adding to the price of beautiful linens. Across Europe, people begin assembling tabletop and bed linens for a baby girl's *trousseau* the moment she is born. Tradition dictates that the first letter of her name reign on the left and the first letter of her last name on the right. The center awaits the first letter of her future husband's family name.

Opposite: In a guest room as beautifully furnished as the home's master bedroom, an antique French bed is elegantly dressed in vintage lace linens—extolled from table and bed linens. Lace curtains are Jack Lenor Larsen.

Elegant linens from Leontine Linens, New Orleans, become even more chic when monogrammed.
Opposite: A träverstin wrapped in vintage lace.

Les Détails

In the seventeenth century, Louis XIV and his visionary finance minister, Jean-Baptist Colbert, established a strictly controlled guild system that regulated the work of artisans, raising the specialties at which they excelled to even higher standards.

The epic scale of this master bedroom requires oversized furnishings, starting with the limestone fireplace, or cheminee, as the French call it.

More than three centuries later, the Sun King perfectionism remains his extraordinary gift to France, though his penchant for extravagance may be better known.

While the latter legacy may always endure, King Louis XIV deserves credit for influencing most everything the French do. From their insistence on finely crafted furniture and regal textiles to turning out rooms with dignity and panache, the French attention to detail, which borders on obsession, is a testimony to the late king's fastidiousness and in keeping with his visions.

In truth, the French leave no creative idea unimplemented in hopes of making their living quarters special. Whether selecting quality leather for a chair or replacing door hardware, the attention to minutiae is striking.

Finely etched knobs, surface bolts, and crémone bolts that could almost pass for artwork bestow added nobility on groaning doors and tall, narrow windows. Crisp crown moldings, seamlessly woven, step out onto ceilings, making spaces appear even taller than they actually are. Polished brass grilles with scrolled motifs adorn heating vents, elevating the ordinary. Bullion is deep rather than shallow, giving upholstery a more sophisticated look. The trims embellishing vintage textiles fabricated into throw pillows are full, not skimpy, illustrating that doubling is key to winning acclaim.

Whereas small paintings would disappear on generous walls, grouped with mirrors and wall sconces, they make a strong statement. Meanwhile, heroic-sized family portraits add splendor and historic character.

Disregarding the American practice of leaving eight to eighteen inches of exposed wood around the perimeter of a room, ample-sized area rugs cross boundary lines, making smaller carpets appear skimpy—and rooms look larger than they are. Even in close quarters, the French think big, opting for a few furnishings—always exaggerated in size—rather than modestly scaled.

Further suggesting the sophistication of a bygone era, several rock-crystal chandeliers may drift overhead in the same room, while shaded sconces wash walls with light, picture lights cast a soft glow, and table and floor lamps direct glare. Together they maneuver light into producing drama and warmth not attainable with overhead light sources. To be sure, the

Sharing the French love for simplicity and beauty, the home-owner opts for a Roman shade beneath master bedroom curtains.

A detail of the leading edge.

French shy away from track lighting, which can jarringly cast unforgiving shadows on the face.

Truth is, it is not as if any list can claim to be exhaustive. But attention to detail is a testament to France's artistic past. Also, it glorifies the memory of the Sun King, whose influence is still felt these hundreds of years later.

ACKNOWLEDGMENTS

Without question, writing a design book can be a struggle, so it never hurts to have help. For those who rallied to make this book possible, I am sincerely grateful.

Dallas sales representative John Smither tracked down Scalamandré's leopard silk velvet—coveted for the front jacket—and had it in the skilled hands of Jesus Marroquin sooner than imagined. The next day, Mike Williams delivered a freshly upholstered chair to the spot where Dan Piassick would photograph it. Hours later, a transparency was on its way to Gibbs Smith, Publisher, accompanied by one for the back jacket with a tale that included borrowing floral designer Judy Blackman's pampered pet.

Meanwhile, homeowners Minnie Doghterty, Allison and Douglas O'Briant, Terry and Ronald Unkefer, (and more), along with designers John Kidd, Rita Madden, Barbara McCutchin, Punita Valambhia and Deborah Walker were priming sites for Dan Piassick and Janet Lenzen's spotlights. I thank them all for a certain *je ne sais quoi* that eludes easy definition.

Thank you, too, to Muriel Abeger, Bruno de la Croix Vaubois, Mary Beth Riddle, and Nicole Zarr for always being so supportive of my projects. And to David Sutherland for the privilege of introducing the "Louis Soleil Collection" of innovative upholstered outdoor furniture.

Deserving of thanks, too, are my assistants, Janice Pedersen Stuerzl and Tara Kohlbacher.

The pages that follow are also the result of the efforts of editor Madge Baird, whose interest, talent, and dedication helped shape this book in addition to my other books in this series, and book designer extraordinaire Cherie Hanson. Thanks also to editorial production associate Melissa Barlow.

Is it any wonder, then, that many people breathed a collective sign of relief when *Secrets of French Design* went to press? Or that I indeed thank Marty Lee, vice president of production at Gibbs Smith, for seeing that bound books arrived in a timely fashion? And Dennis Awsumb and Kellie Robles for helping them find their way to you? Still, my guess is that everyone mentioned knows that it never hurts to have help!

Opposite: Elsewhere in the room shown on page 6 stands the Waldo Fernandez daybed, wearing a Jacque Bouvet et Cie linen. The eighteenth-century French armoire is pearwood

DIRECTORY OF DESIGNERS

Here is where to find the designers whose work appears in this book.

John Kidd, Allied Member ASID
Punita Valambhia
John Kidd Associates
5120 Woodway Road
Suite 7033
Houston, Texas 77056
Telephone: 713.961.1912

Rita Madden
Ashburn Act II
2121 Kirby Drive
Suite 11 NW # 38
Houston, Texas 77019
Telephone 713.528.2805

Barbara J. McCutchin
Barbara J. McCutchin
Interior Design
4516 Lovers Lane
Suite 449
Dallas, Texas 75225
Telephone 214.528.6478

Betty Lou Phillips, ASID
Interiors by BLP
4278 Bordeaux Avenue
Dallas, Texas 75205
Tel.214.599.0191

Deborah Walker & Associates
1925 Cedar Springs Road,
Suite 103
Dallas, Texas 214.521.9637

DESIGNER CREDITS

John Kidd, Allied Member ASID,
68, 70
Punita Valambhia

Rita Madden, 15, 25, 50, 54, 56, 62,
65

Barbara J. McCutchin, 10, 20, 44

Betty Lou Phillips, ASID, cover,
back jacket

Deborah Walker, ASID, 49

PHOTOGRAPHIC CREDITS

Janet Lenzen, 9, 15, 25, 32, 35, 36,
40, 50, 54, 56, 62, 65, 68, 70

Dan Piassick, cover, back jacket,
title page, opposite copyright, con-
tents page, 10, 20, 23, 44, 49, 53, 55,
59, 72, 75, 77

COMPLIMENTARY PHOTOGRAPHS

Christofle Silver, 61

David Sutherland, Inc. (Ka Yeung,
photographer), 16, 78

Leontine Linens
(Sarah Essex, photographer), 71

From the "Louis Soleil Collection" for Sutherland is outdoor furniture designed by John Hutton. Fabric is Perennials' Mosaic.